Mannequin Designs

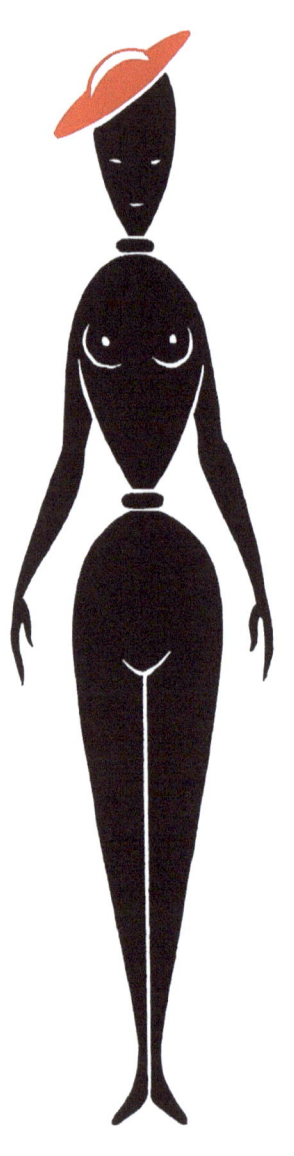

Mannequin Designs

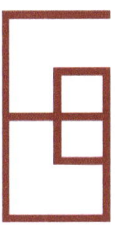

Gavin L. O'Keefe

2018

First published 2011
Revised edition 2018

Art © 2018

Gavin L. O'Keefe
PO Box 571
Lavington NSW 2641
Australia

ISBN 978-1461036456

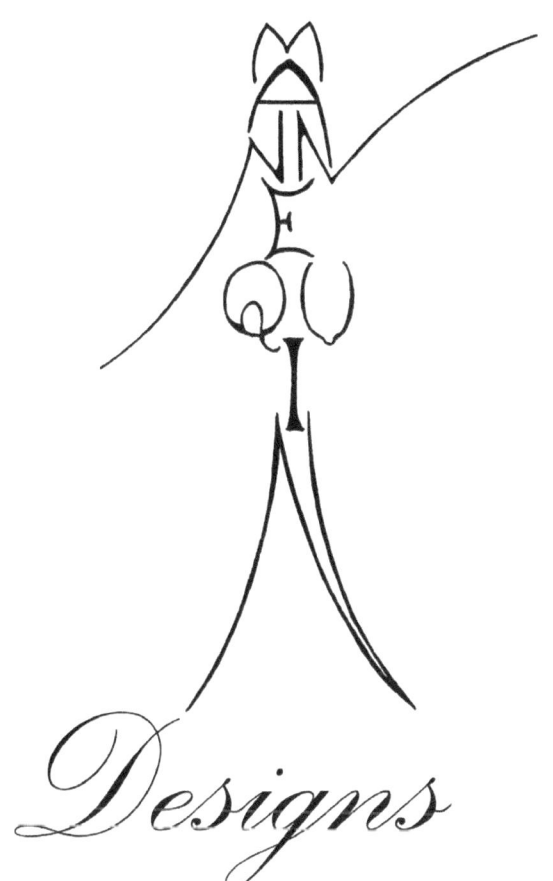

Designs

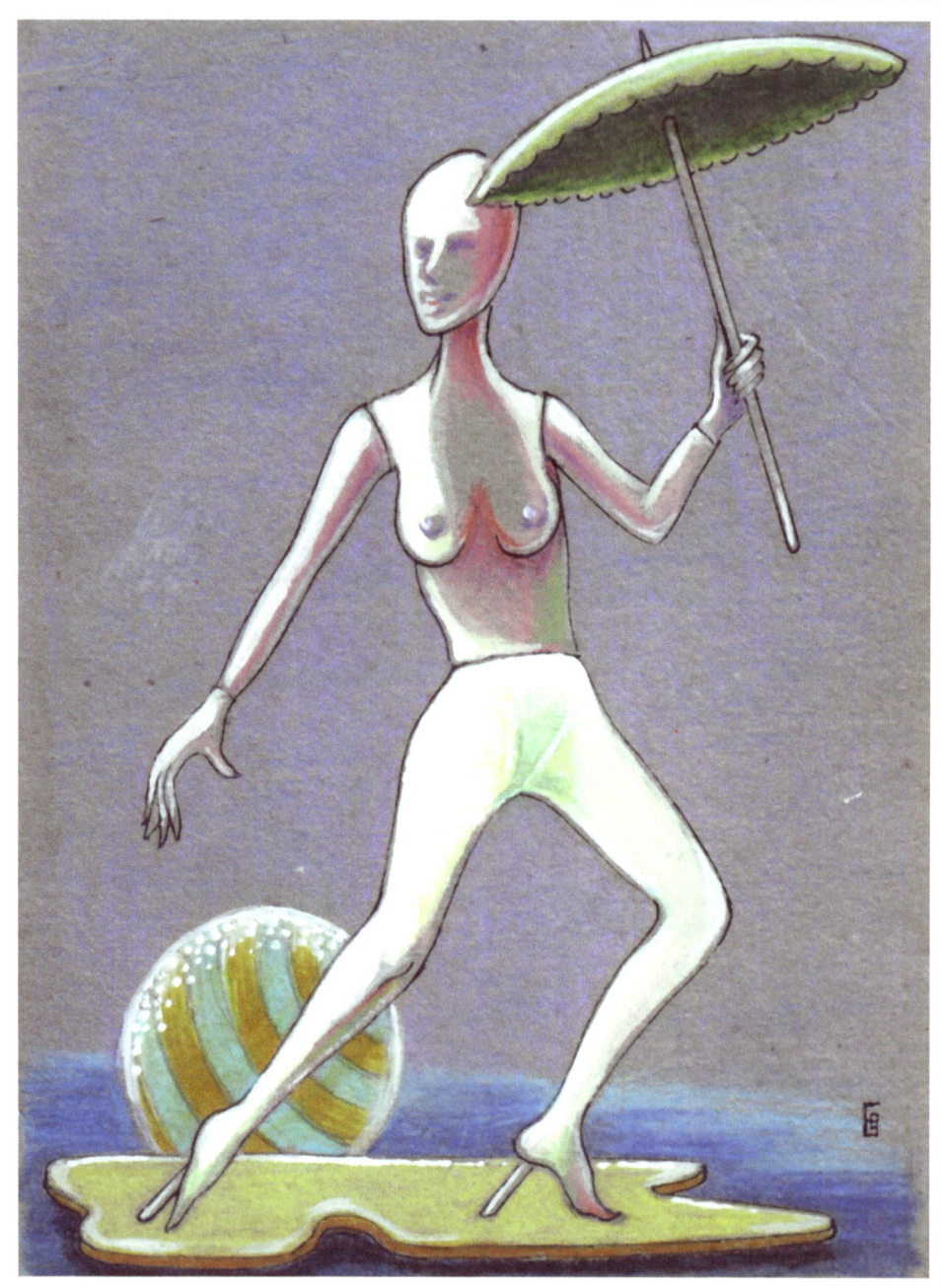

Seaside Frolic

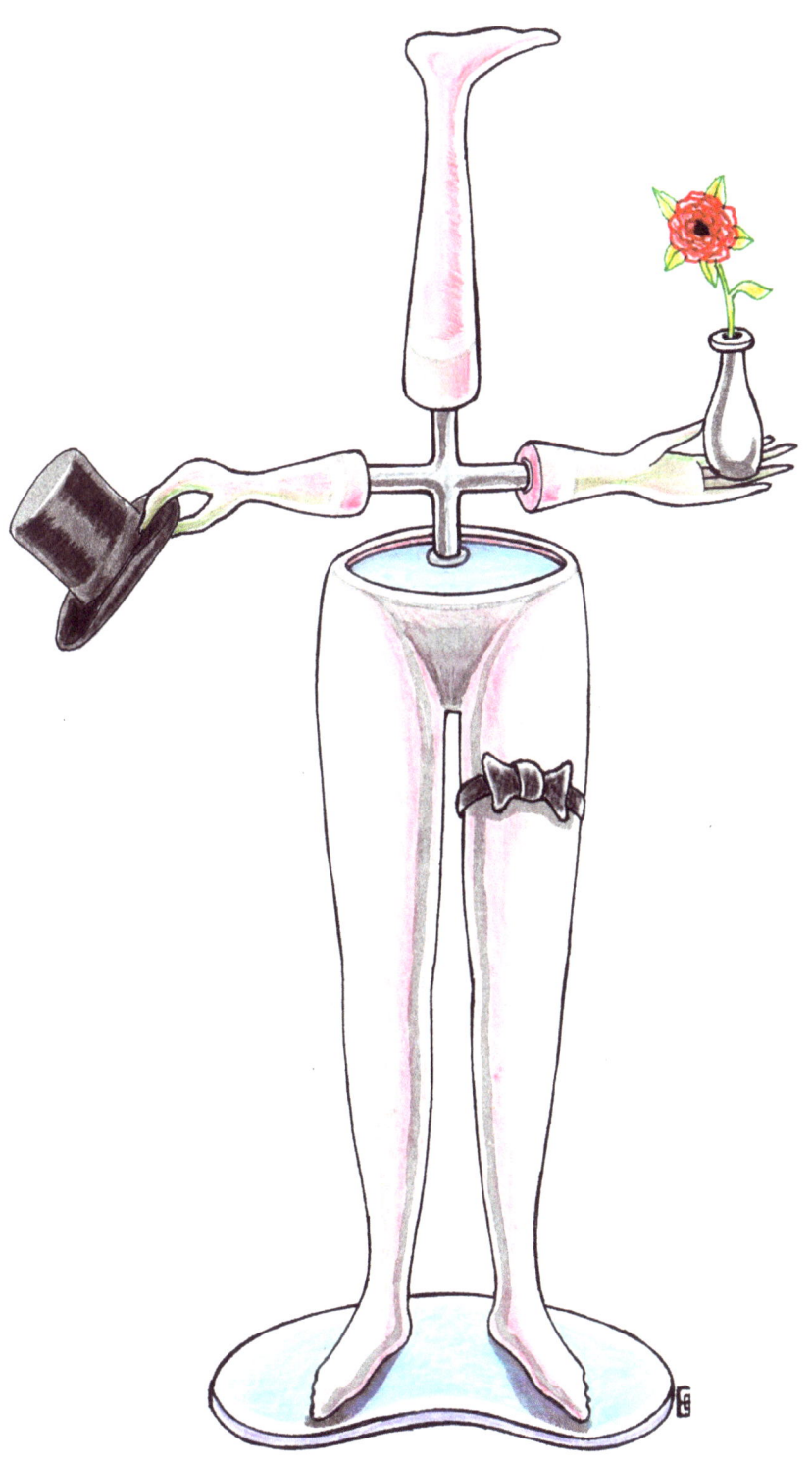

Balance

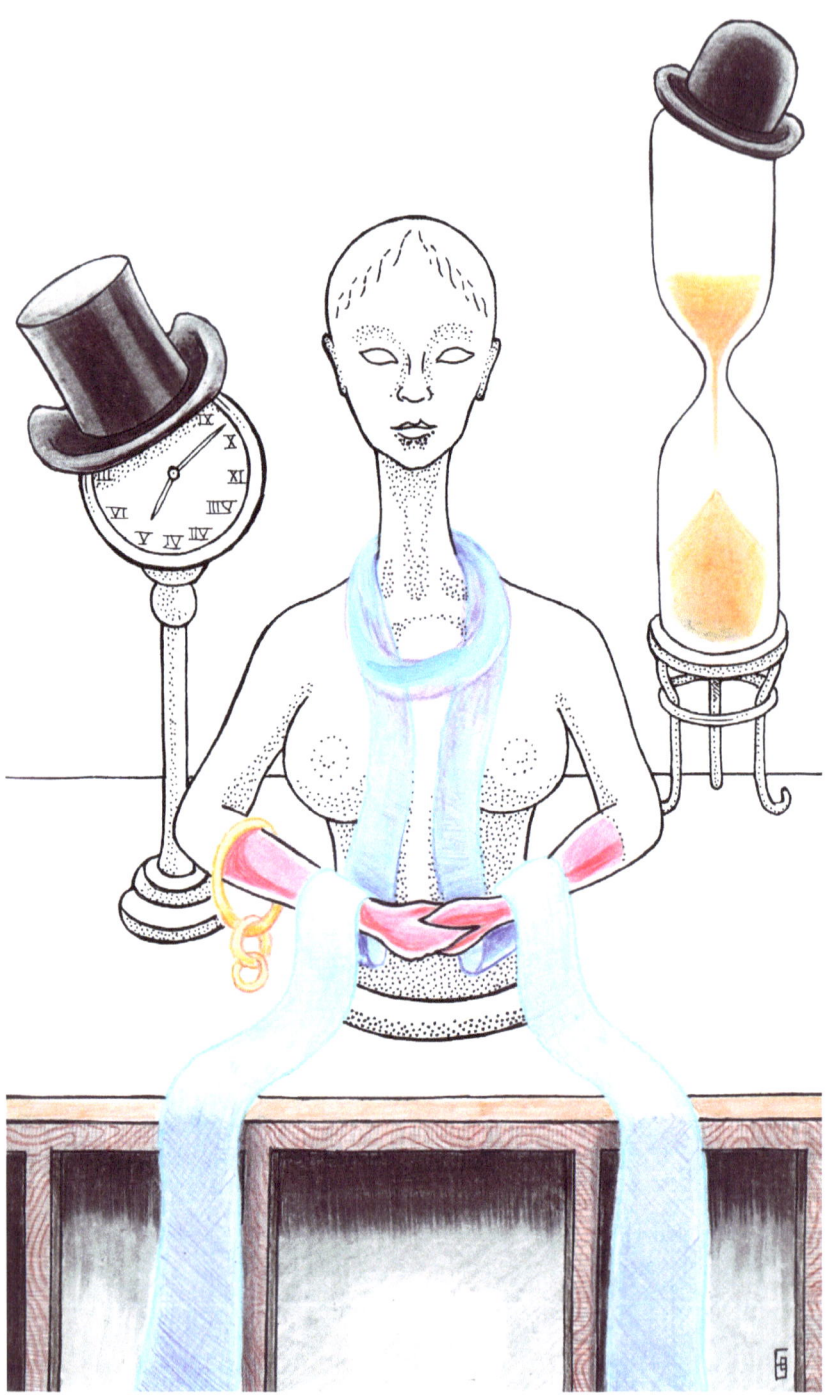

Silk

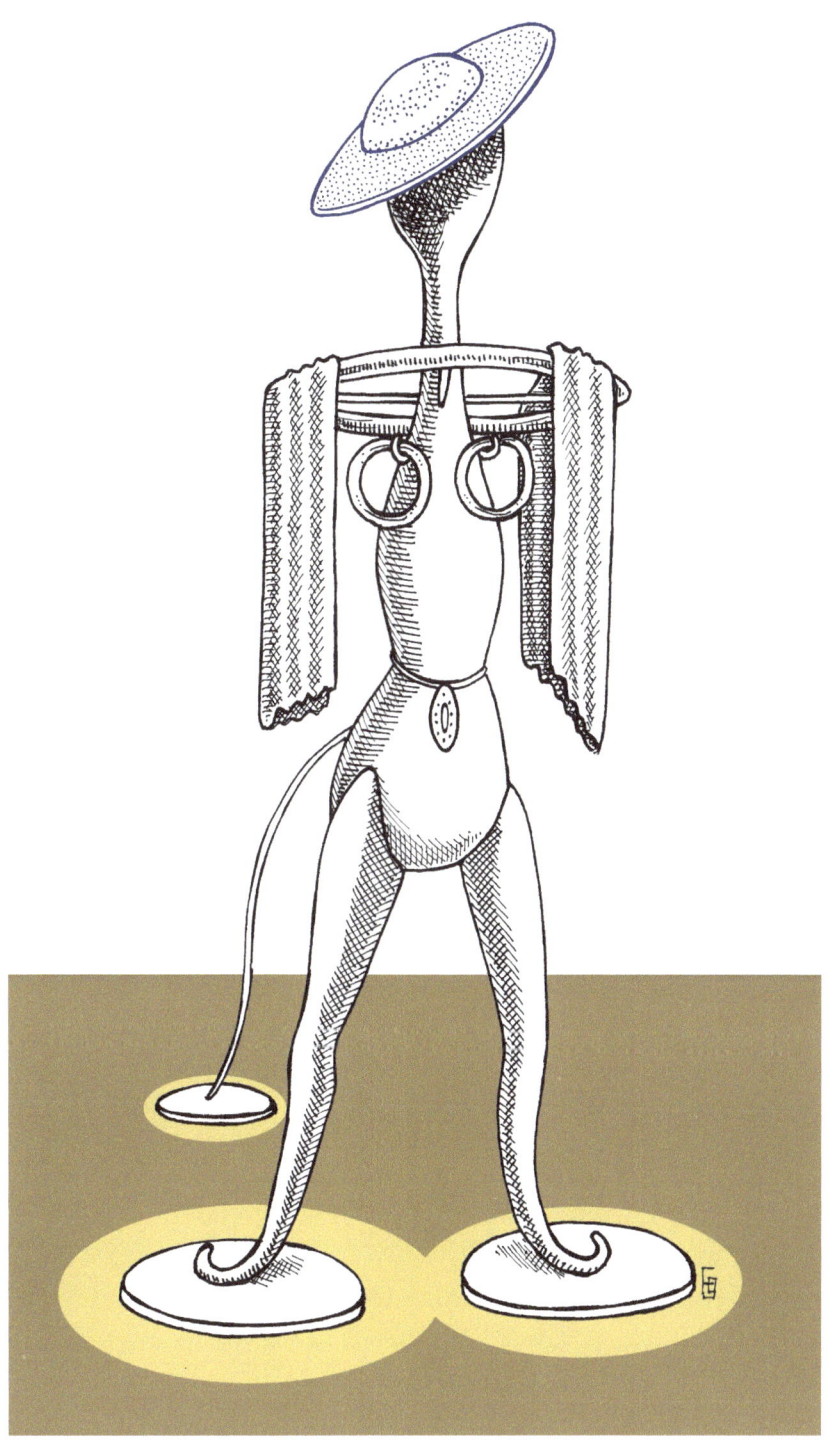

Tripod

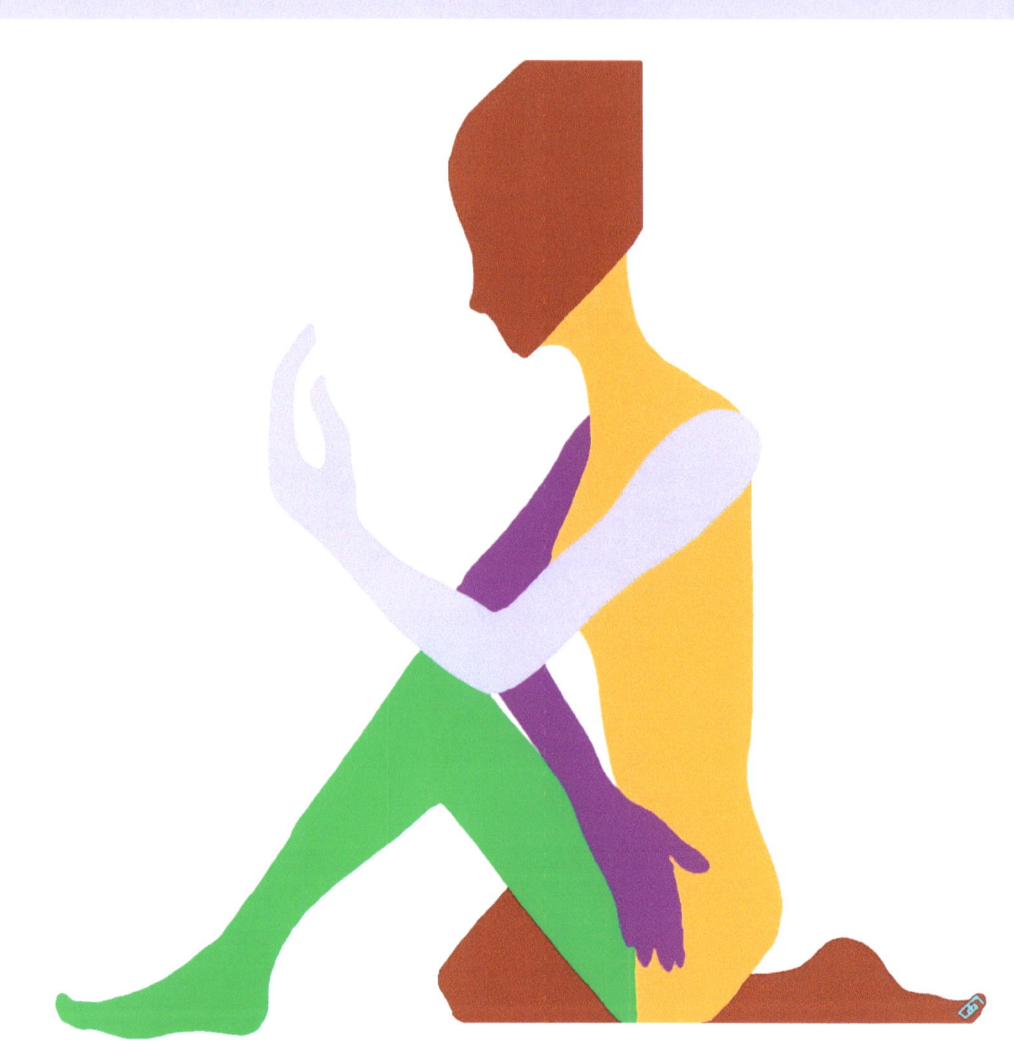

Harlequin

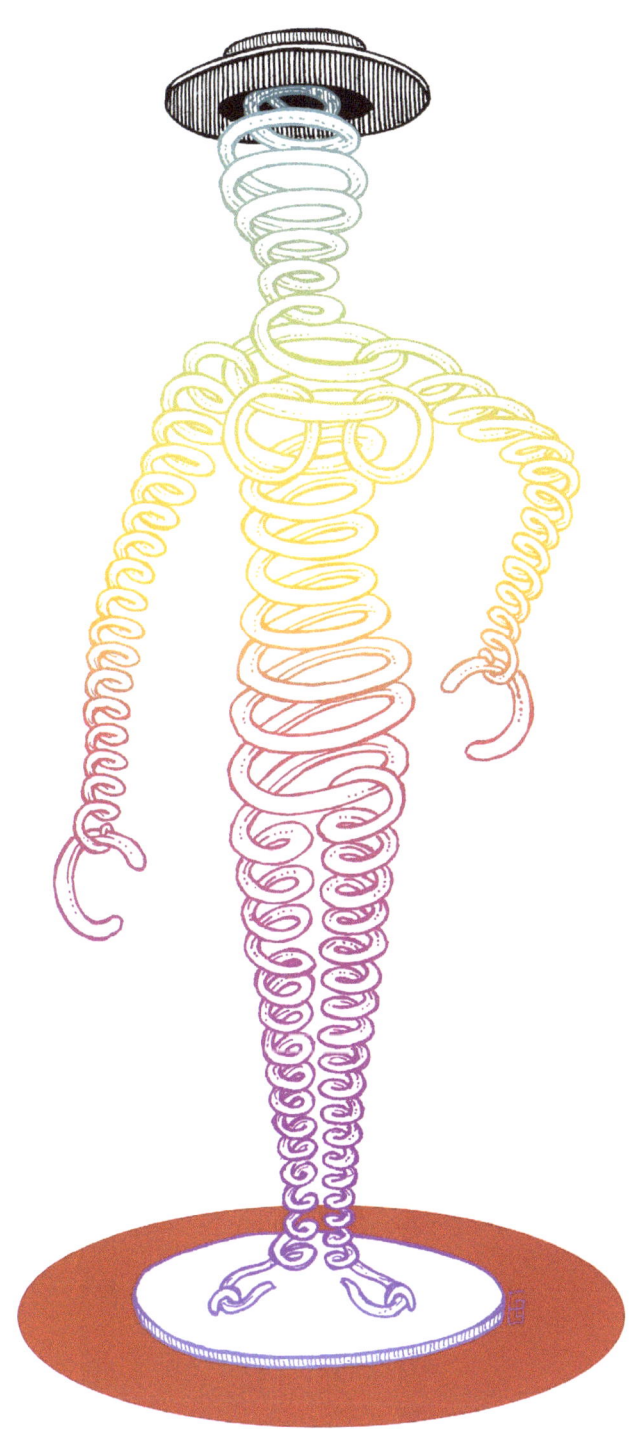

Spring Sale

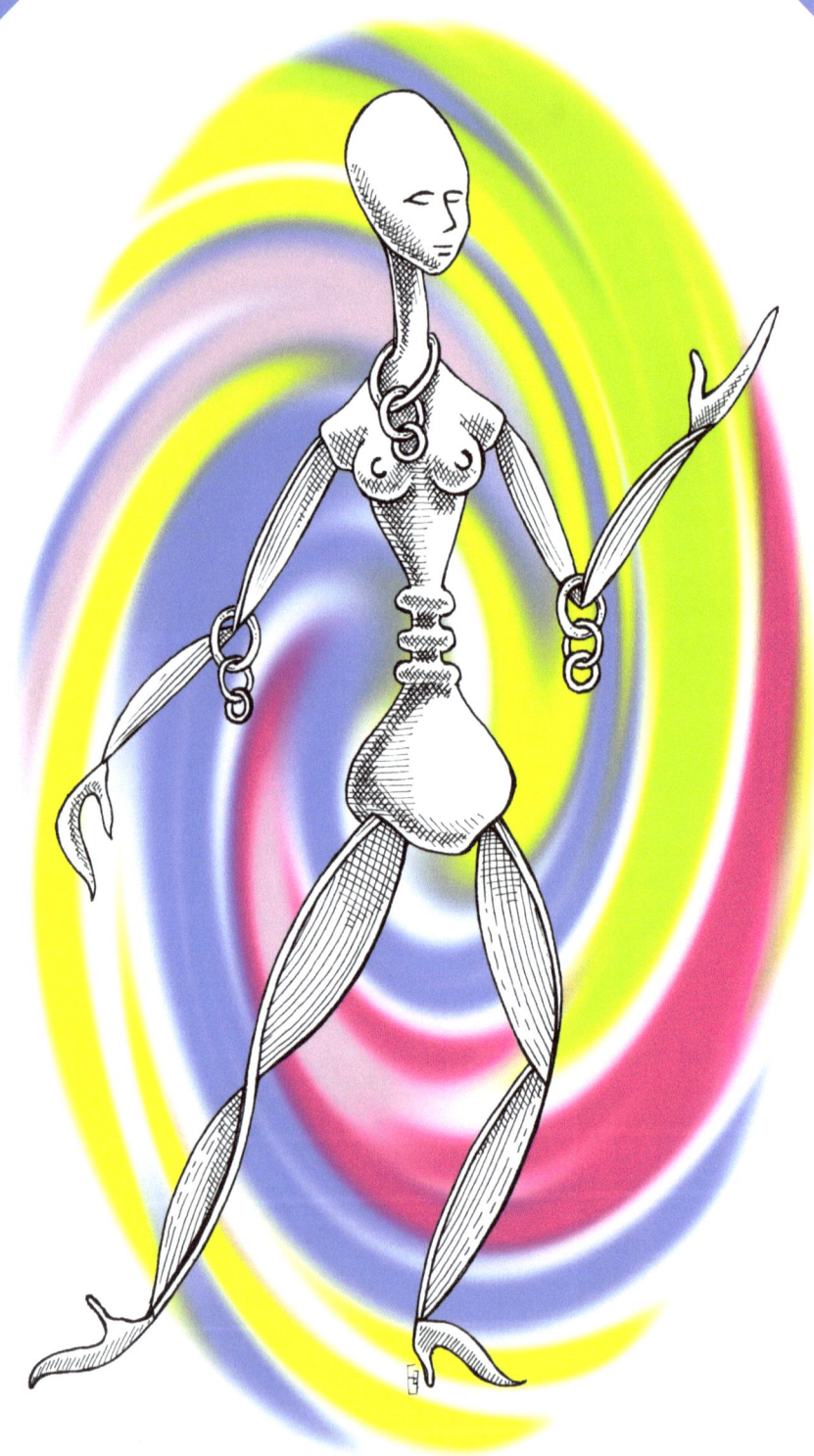

Flares

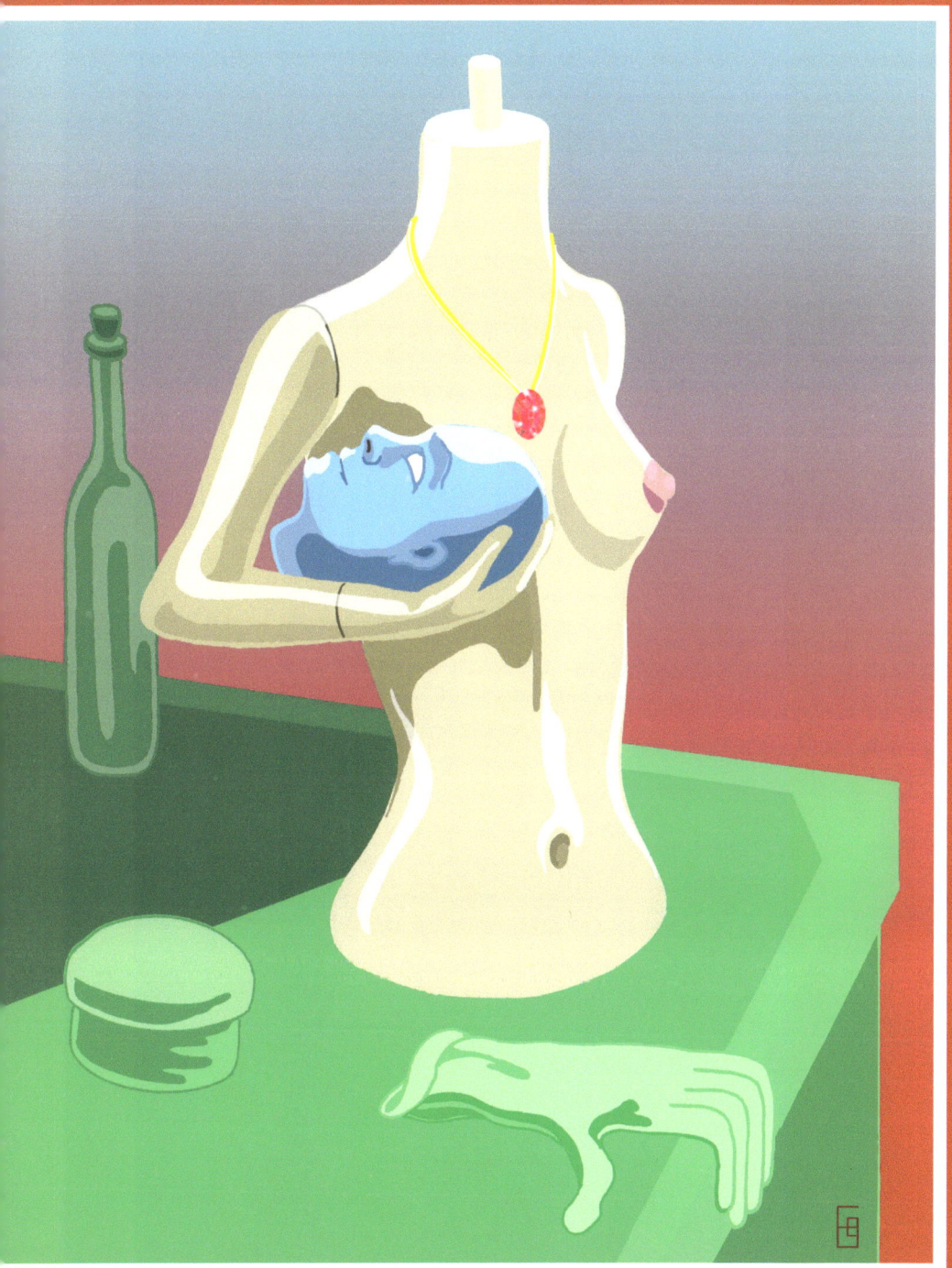

The Blues

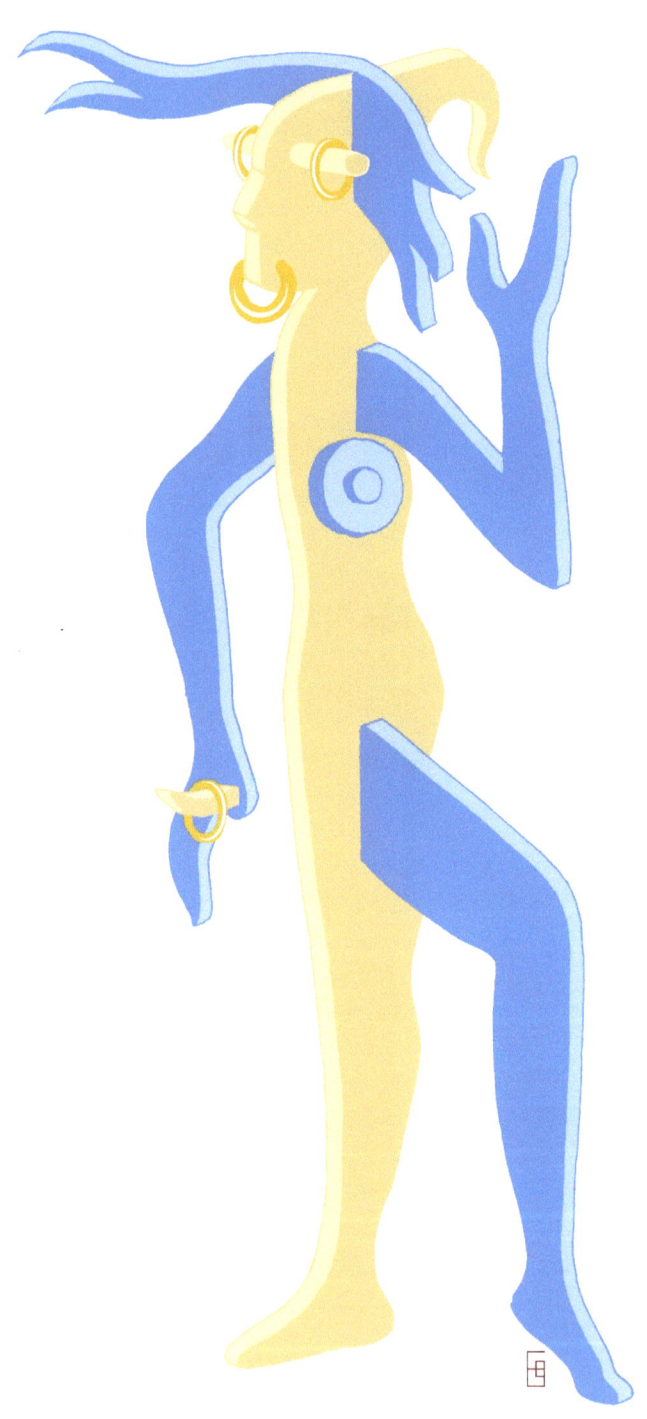

3D

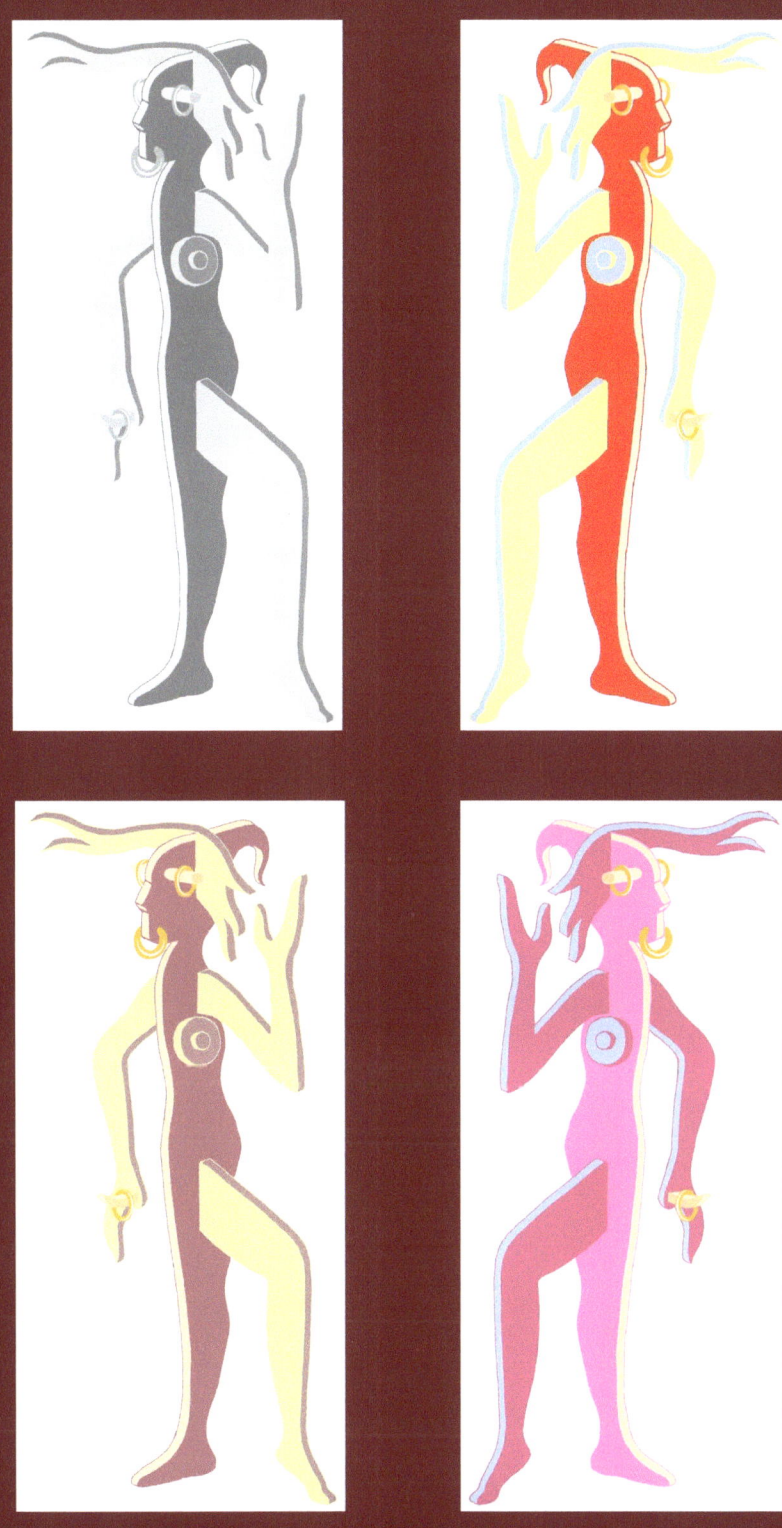

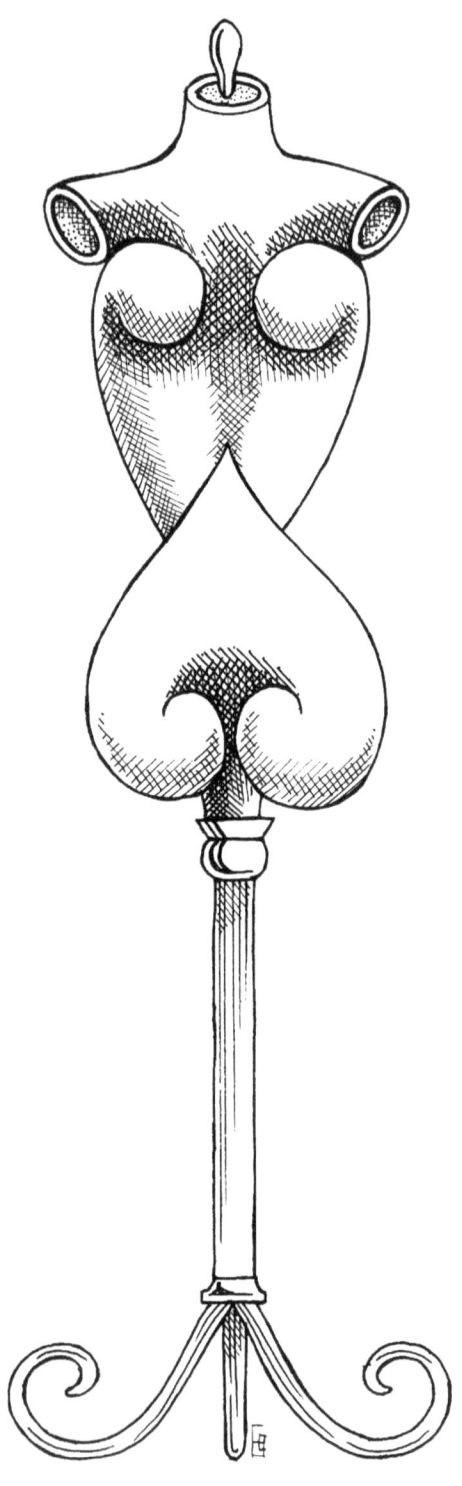

Simplicity

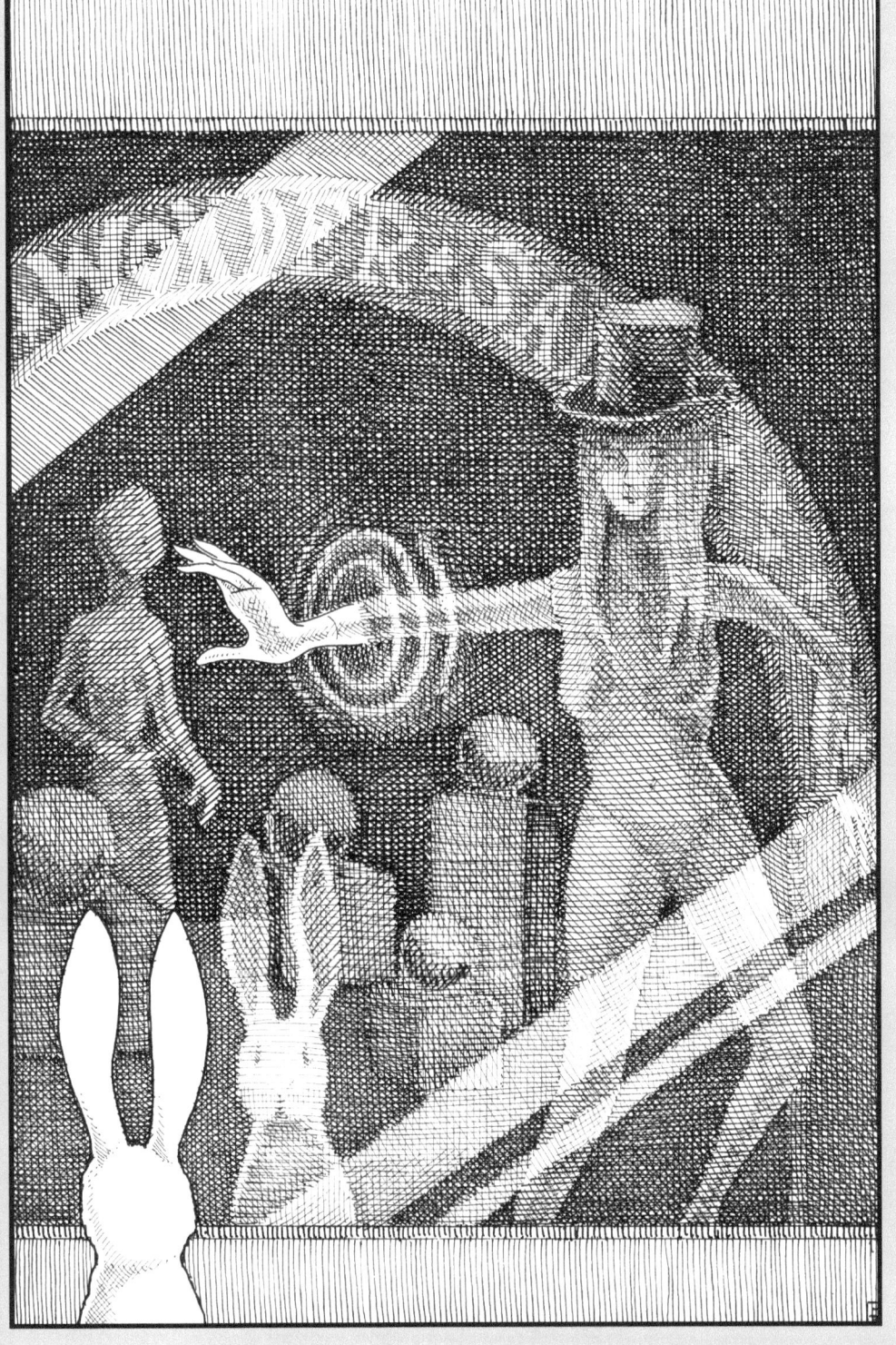

Through the Looking-Glass

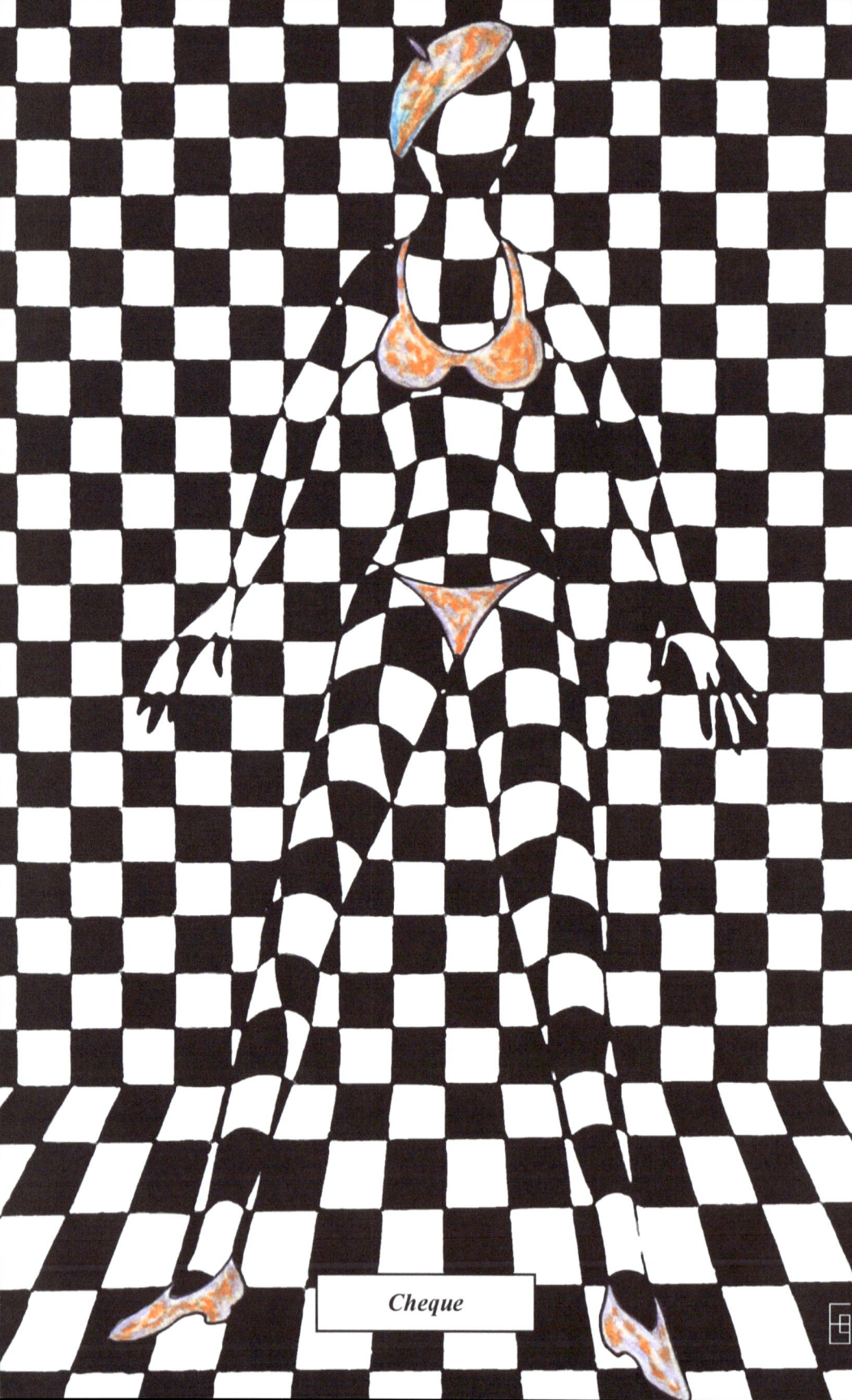

Cheque

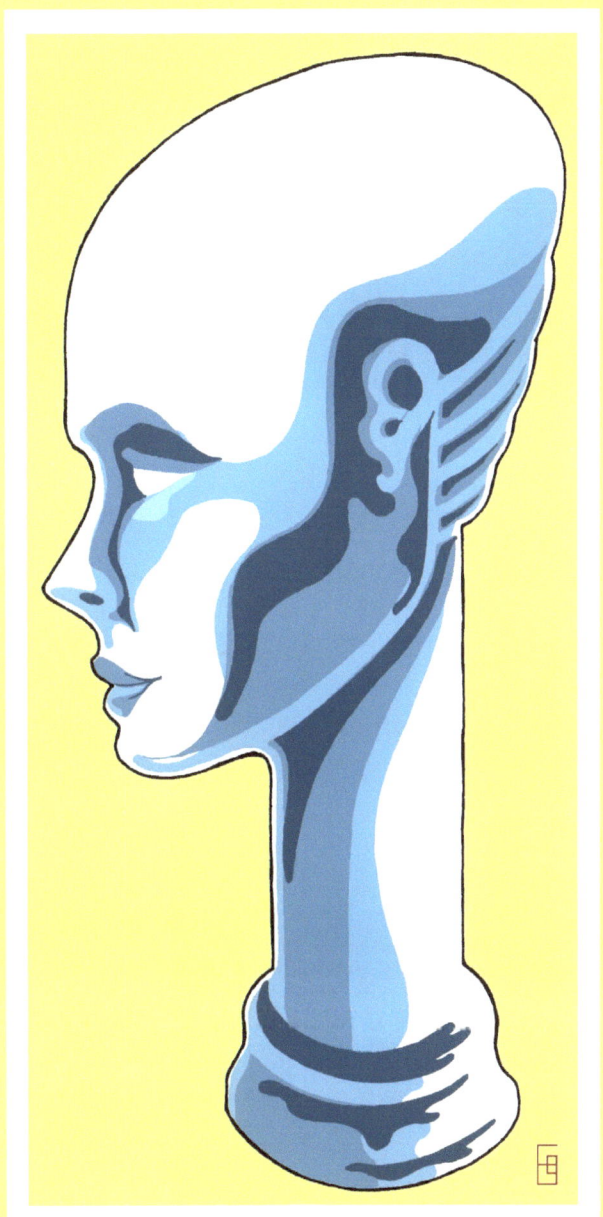

Profile

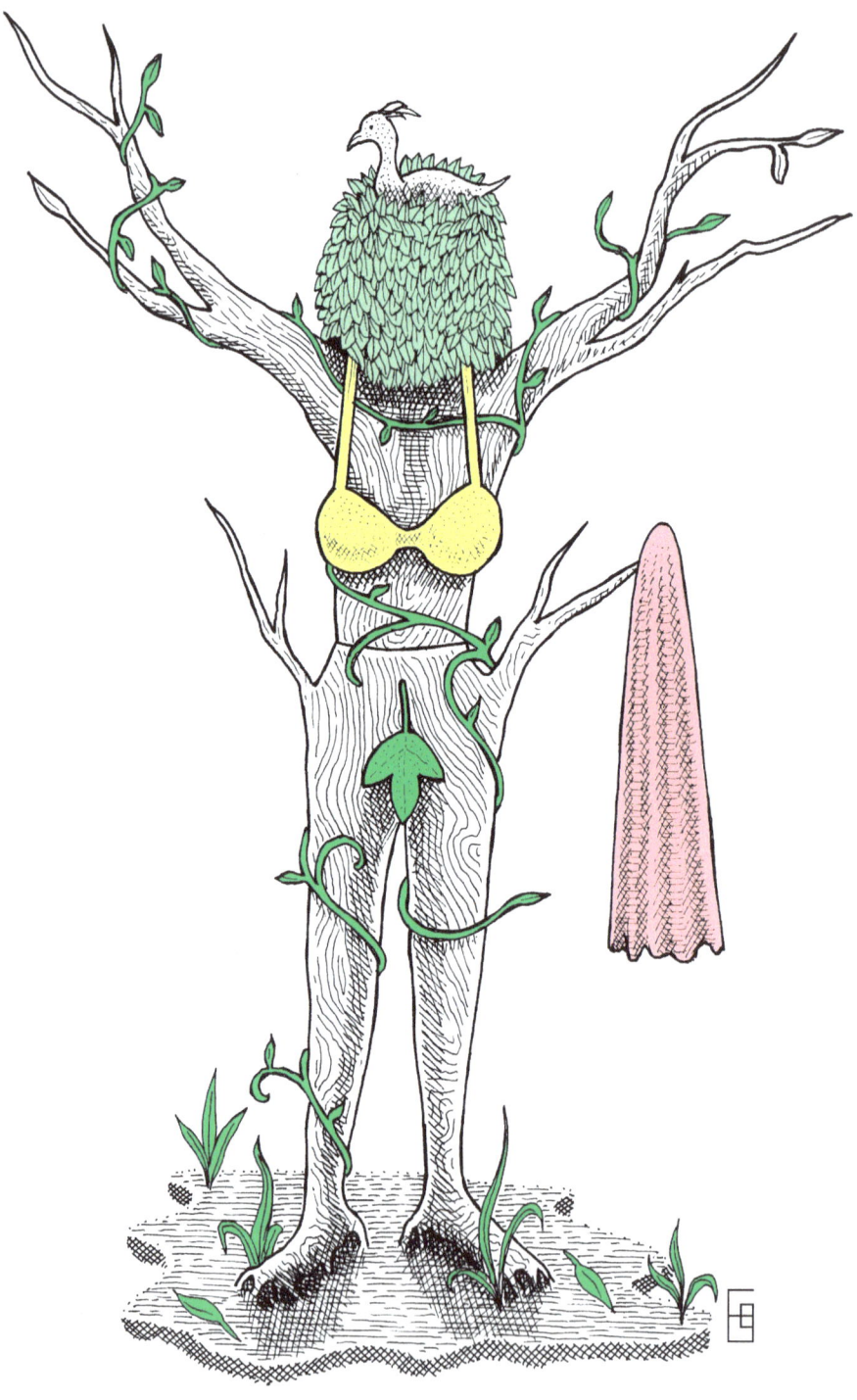

Fall Sale

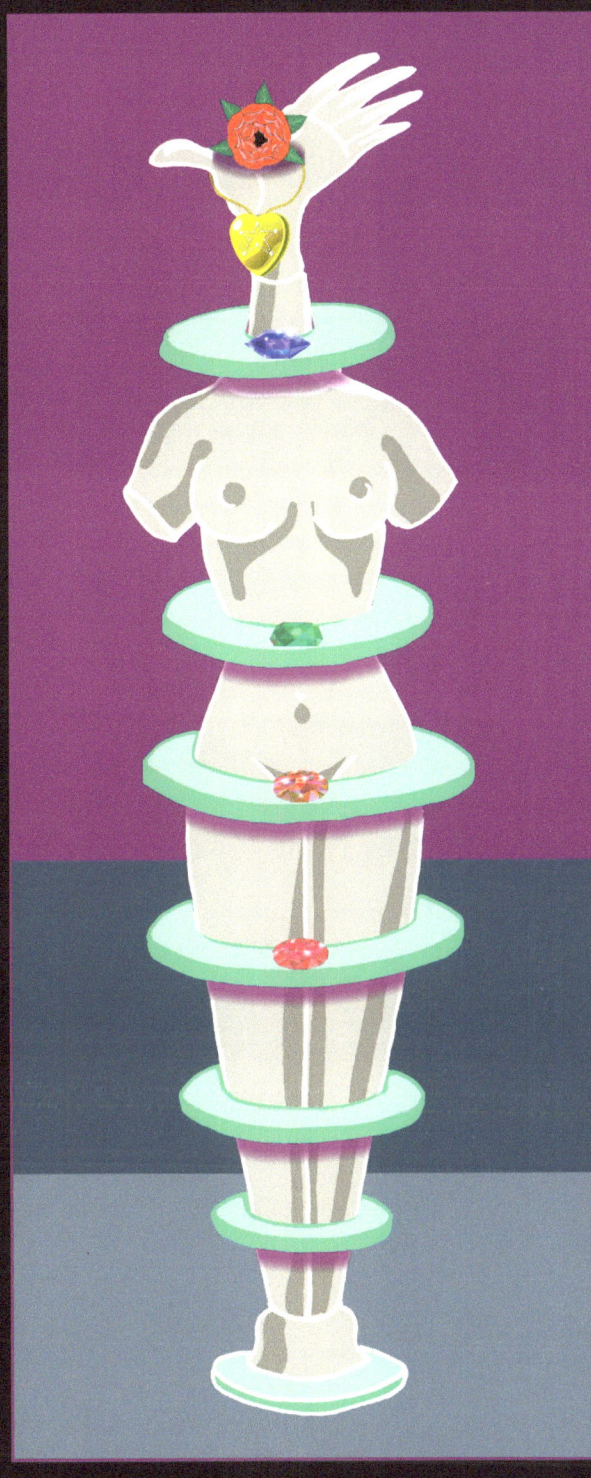

Jewellery Display

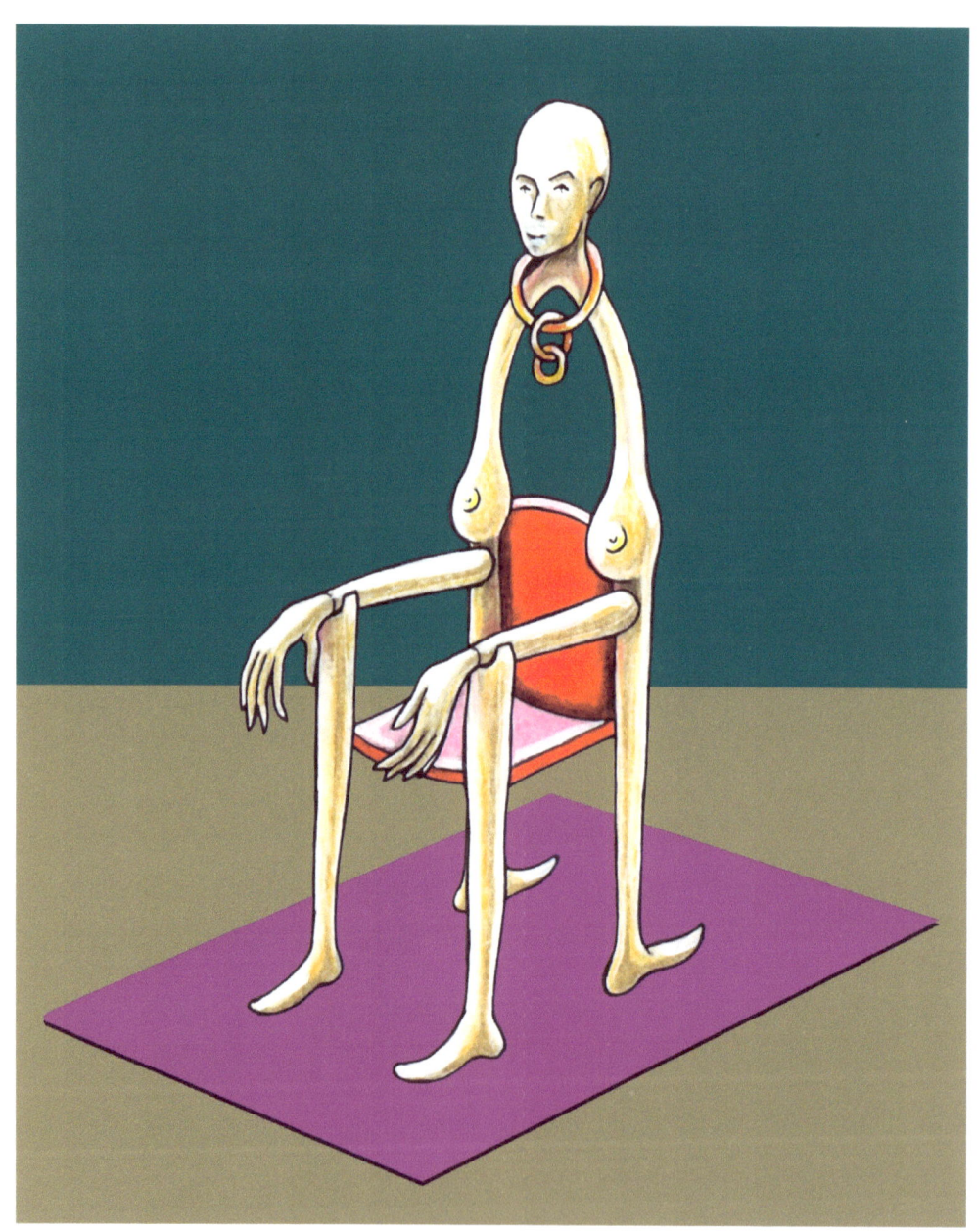

Armchair

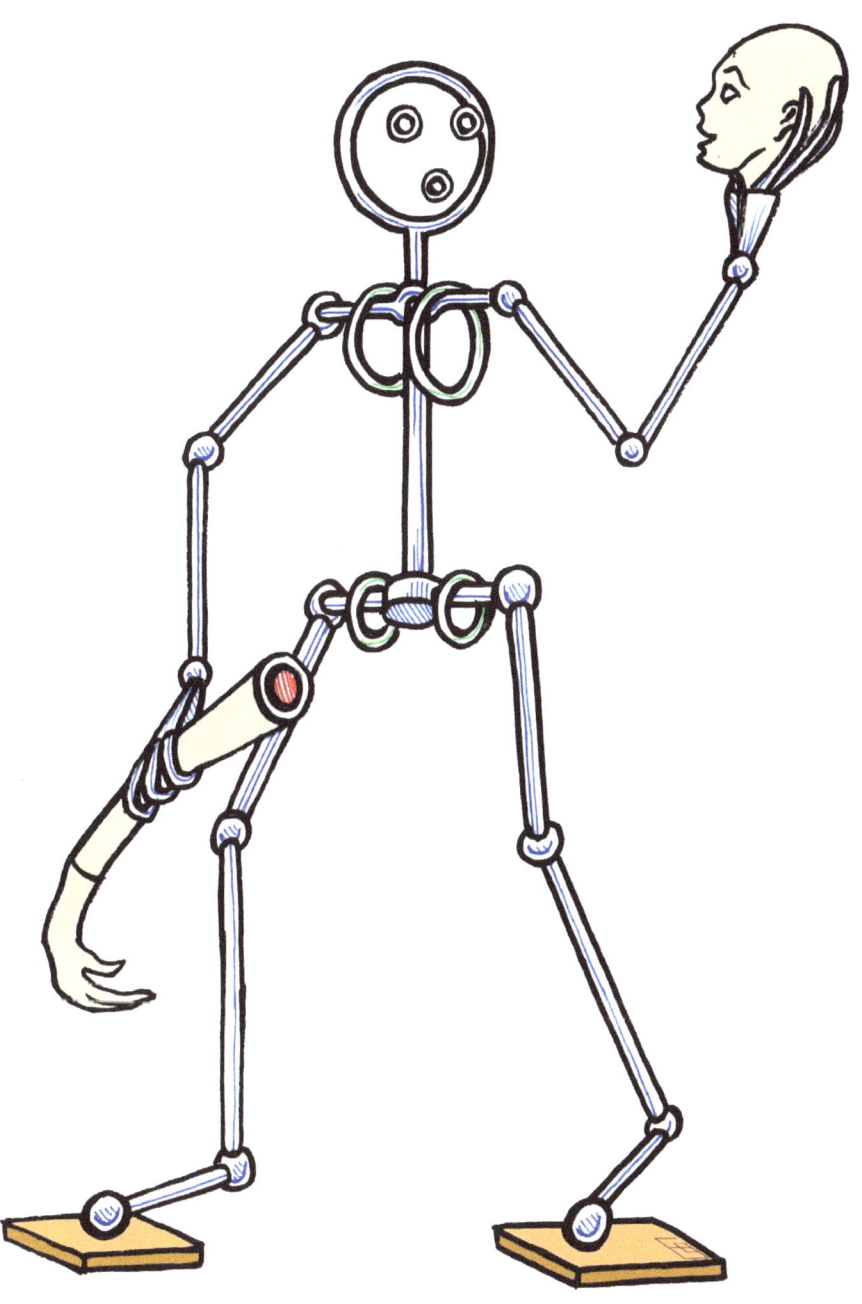

Stick Figure

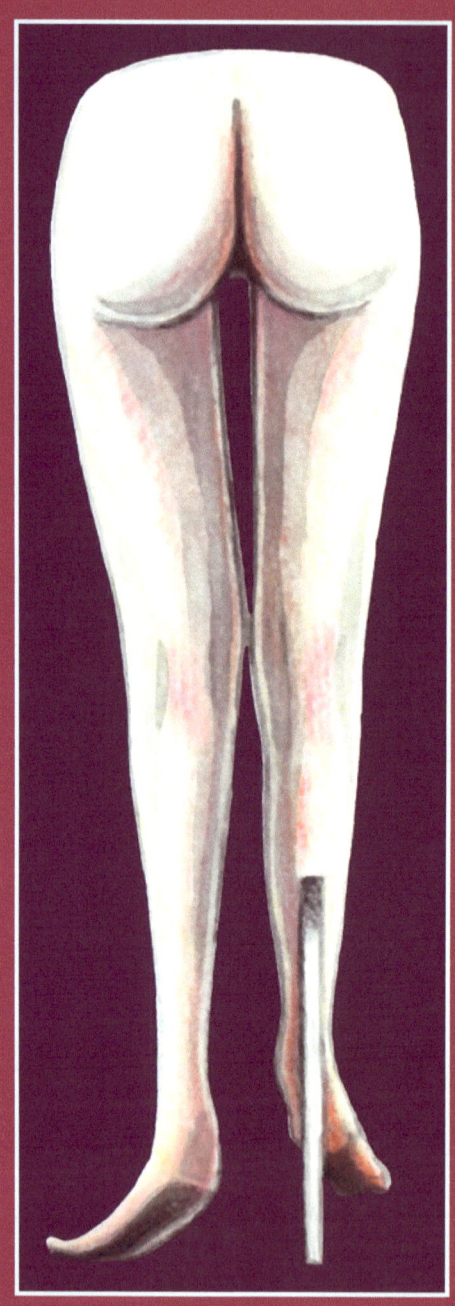

The End